Carrying Stones

Photos & Poems by Nicoline Evans

THE BLUEST BIRD

It came to me in a dream.
I am farther away than I seem.
Find me where the end becomes someplace new; a place for me without you.
Where the bottom rises and delivers a pulse;
turn my nothingness into something beautiful.

Mt. Walker, Washington

CHASING GHOSTS

I walk down the lonely road searching for the goodbyes I never received.
Silence greets me as I kick up dirt and dust,
and the buzzing fly circling my head begins to sound like a familiar voice.
The sun is playing tricks on me again.
I start to sense that I will not find a pulse, but I continue my search.
A heartbeat. A whimper. Anything to prove I'm not alone,
to prove that life resumes in my brokenness.
But the desert is unkind to the wandering mind and I find myself scorched and defeated.
"Farewell," I shout.
"Farewell," the desert echoes back.
The words I always needed, I give to myself.

Devil's Highway, U.S. 491, New Mexico

Sunrise in Utah

ALL THAT'S LEFT

You recoil, cringing at the sight of me.
I recoil, lost in who I used to be.
My only friends, with me till the end
clinging to the person I never want to be again.
I try to let go, but this is all I know.
I swallow the key.
Buried deep, this is the only secret left to keep.

QUIET

All I lost gave life to what was found:
Alone,
awake,
alive
—this silence is my favorite sound.

THE SPIRAL

I cannot see past my fingertips; what I built is no longer mine.
I claw at my eyes.
A scratch, a scrape, I'm blind;
long gone is the clarity I once wished to find.
I reach.
Afraid of what I might find if I try.
Relief:
The dirt under my nails proves that I haven't lost this fight.
I claw, I scrape, I climb,
determined to reclaim the undefined.
The dirt under my nails is proof I fought to survive.

Ireland

WHEN IT COMES

The morning screams a deafening cry and I awake with a jump.
I am covered in lies.
Another round of swinging arms, circling the clock like there's nothing to hide.
But I am losing time, I'm losing space, I'm losing my chance to recover with grace.
Sun to sky and moon to dirt, I search for the light, but I keep getting burnt.
I think of you when my hollow bones hurt. I wait for the day when my words will be heard.
This night has caught fire by the disappearing sun.

Readington, New Jersey

Grand Cayman Island

VICARIOUSLY

Hey, friend, I was wondering where you've been.
Haven't seen you since the red sun rose and stole your heart again.
Are you lost at sea? Did you find some peace down there?
Will the tides lead you home, or will you learn to live without air?
I suppose a missing heart is a treasure worth finding,
but I wonder if you'll lose yourself before you ever find it.
I look to the clouds and wonder if you're there;
Safe with your missing piece and dreaming of elsewhere.
Have you filled the hole? Have you recovered what they stole?
Or have you learned to be whole by letting go?
I wonder for you, and I wonder for me.
To continue, or abandon, this hunt for my missing piece.

INTO THE NIGHT

Gone beyond the wicked evening sun—
the warmth that leaves as fast as it comes.
I try to hide the way such goodbyes leave me cold,
and every time the light departs I am reminded why I must go.
So I fly, away from this and that; the tiny realities to which I cannot grasp.
If I run, I need never stop.
If I leave, I'll never know what I lost.

Lubec, Maine

Grand Cayman Island

THE LAST DANCE

There's a fire lighting the way, trying to guide me offshore,
but I linger in the dark—those flames have burned me once before.
I cling to the sight of it, the flickering, sickening pulse of it, beckoning me to follow.
In the cold, I know what waits for me: a monster who swallows me whole, spits out my
bones, then does it once more.
In the warmth awaits the unknown—the final dance with my greatest foe.
I won't go.
I've grown to love the devil I know.

SILENCE

For all the words I've said, the ones locked in my head scream loudest.

Alstede Farm, Chester, NJ

THE BUILDER

A stone for your troubles, it's all I have.
I'm drowning, in fact,
in dirt and sediment.
I could build a castle, or a secret hideaway,
crafted from the stones the others threw my way.
Better because of all the weight they made me carry.
Happy despite endless attempts to leave me buried.
The others will see me touch the sun.
The others will hear me howl at the moon.
They will wonder how I learned to fly while carrying their stones;
I suspect the others never thought I'd make those stones my home.

Round Valley Reservoir, Clinton, New Jersey

HALFWAY

Between here and there, I'm blurred.
Gone, but not forgotten.
Lost in the static of what I've been and who I wish to be.
If you hear my frantic whispers amidst the rushing wind,
please be kind.
We are creatures of light clawing through the darkest minds.

Arches National Park, Utah

REDEFINED

Hidden between the seams of where I'm ripped up, stitched up, carelessly.
Here, I see the shape of sound. I see every reckless word that ever left your mouth.
You think I'm lost.
I know I'm found.
I fell, but never hit the ground.
Belief in what is yet to be; I dream in colors never seen.

EVERGREEN

Found my way through the evergreens.
Left step, right. Again, on repeat.
My feet keep pace with the forest's heartbeat.
Thudding soles on the beaten path,
I'm on my way, but I'm not there yet.
Left turn, right. A pause; I'm lost.
Weaving maze of limbs brush me free at last.
Ahead, I charge through the evergreens.
Found, I leave behind the worst of me.

Jasper National Park, Alberta, Canada

EVERYTHING

I made you up in my head.
A face, a place, the way you kept me safe.
Another monster to play with my imaginary friends.
Wildfire scorches the depths: one, two, three till there's nothing left but me.
I'll keep you safe—buried in the graveyard where wildflowers spread.
I made you up in my head.
Sun-kissed petals bloom over the darkest regret.
I've made something out of nothing again.

Jasper National Park, Alberta, Canada

THE NOWHERE LOVE

While the flowers remain, I take one step forward.
Winter arrives.
I take one step back.
I can hardly remember your face,
still I'm trapped in this place.
Teetering between the fickle seasons of your love.

Herring Cove, Campobello Island, New Brunswick, Canada

Spruce Run Reservoir, Clinton, New Jersey

HAUNTED

Tattered by a love never given,
shattered by your broken heart's rhythm.
I thought I killed you, but you won't leave.
The worst kind of death is the kind that still breathes.

TRUSTFALL

I sway.
This way and that.
You fade.
In and out.
Down the line and curved, everything is different, I am not me anymore.
I twirl, taking with me your breath.
You gasp, giving to me all you have left.
Up and away, blazed and gleaming, taller than the sky;
intoxicated by the way your arrival gave me life.
I plummet, body racing the wind, finally ready for the fall.
But you aren't there to catch me.
You were never there at all.
And there is no return for the forgotten after they've hit the ground.
Another end delivered where so many beginnings were found.

Sulphur Skyline, Jasper National Park, Alberta, Canada

Cutler Cove, Maine

BLEEDING BLUES

Where are you, my bluest blue?
Once by my side through the thickest sorrows, now gone from every waking tomorrow.
Both cause and effect, who am I without you?
A ghost of what I've known, of what I've been.
A shadow looking for light to be seen.
I disappear into my yesteryears.
The pull to my push, the hush to my cries.
My only love was the truest lie.
The fix and the fall.
You were my only, afterall.
My bluest blue, I slay the thought of you.
Bleeding blues—the only love I ever knew.

THE CHANGE

Wrapped in sunshine, I'm born anew.
A pause, a breath; this is my truth.
Your storm arrives—I rise above.
No longer will I call it love.

HOVER

Everywhere; in every face, in every song.
I hover, afraid to breathe wrong.
If I move, I might lose what was never mine to hold.
Everywhere, colored in the saddest hues:
I think of me.
I think of you.

Petrified ForestNational Park, Arizona

KNIGHTED

Battered by the beating within my chest;
I am no longer here, no longer there.
A dream in light you will forget
and recall in the moonlight as a nightmare.
Wings clipped, I look different—
you watch my shadow take its crown.
Light pours through my broken bits.
I wonder if you see me now.

POLARIS

Meet me there,
atop the mossy hilled edge
where the northern star kisses eastern winds.
I see you there.
The brightest light in the darkest space.
I am set aflame.

Banff National Park, Alberta, Canada

EXPIRED

Gone are the days of desire.
Now we have sorrow.
Now we have fire.

Acadia National Park, Maine

Moab, Utah

AFTER THE FIRE

Only cinders remain.
I find myself searching the wreckage again.
For a clue, a sign—for proof that anything survived.
Only ashes of the past;
what I loved could never last.
Gone, then back again—a new dawn, another day.
I try to change, but stay the same.
My haunted heart cries for yesterday.
I search the wreckage once again.
Only cinders remain.

DREAMCATCHER

Emerald dreams catch me where I lay.
The good, the bad, and everything lost along the way.
A cluttered web spun recklessly—I count what's missing every day.
One to fifty.
Come what may.
Or so I say while you evaporate.
Within the knotted web I wait
and watch all I've loved slip away.
There is no night without the day.
I'll wait till I am the reason you stay.

Lake O'Hara, Yoho National Park, British Columbia, Canada

East Glacier, Montana

DISTORTED

Hollowed and filled with color to mask the way you left me cold.
Carved and painted over to change the story that was told.
Reflected in the eyes of those who lived to say, "I tried."
Miles of sky as empty as the way you said goodbye.

Williams, Arizona

RUN

I won't go.
I will stay to the end.
Still as stone, your clutch is crippling.
I will wait.
I will see this through.
Till I'm blinded by the very thought of you.
You tell me to leave.
You insist that I go.
But my flight would bring the death of everything I love.
So I stay.
I don't run away,
and I lose you to the moon anyway.

ANYWAY

A siren in my head—this is how it ends.
My morning, my moon, my fading gray.
I loved you yesterday.

Banff National Park, Alberta, Canada

WISH YOU WERE HERE

Droplets for each moment that we hold dear;
the moments we remember through the tears.
I still feel you after all these years—
a whisper in the night only I can hear.

MAYBE NEXT TIME

I see your face in the sky.
Dark clouds, dark eyes, circled by the sorrow we could never fix.
I tried.
I died five times by your side.
Still, I couldn't breathe life back into the friend I once called mine.
And your name—I cringe each time it's uttered by strangers.
The sound of the letters crashing together rattles my bones like thunder.
Your loss, I am buried under.

Ruby Beach, Olympic National Park, Washington

View from Mount Rundle, Banff National Park, Alberta, Canada

TINY FIGHTER

Tiny fighter, I see you there, waiting for the beast to meet your glare.

Hellfire reared and taking aim.

You will not lose.

Not today.

Refusing the hand outstretched from the dark.

Defying the bells that wish to claim your heart.

The shadowy beast calls your name.

It will not win.

Not today.

Air once stolen fills your lungs with life and cushions your wings as you take flight.

Above and beyond the evening glow.

Sometimes you win by letting go.

CHASM

Cratered into what I've done,
a hole replaces all I love.
The unforgiving rise anew
and I'm left with the ghost of you.

Cape Flattery, Washington

Stevens Pass, Washington

COLLISION

When death greets the world, arriving as fast as it departs,
within that space lingers the most crooked of hearts.
Icy veins, freckled soul, and an urge to discover what hides in the unknown.
After life, after death, it craves an existence not discovered yet.
Beyond this world the answers hide, forever evading the curious eye.
But a glimpse can be caught when you watch beauty die
if you're aware that its death means the start of new life.

SAVING DAYLIGHT

I loved you long before the darkness came to stay.
And I'll love you long after you've gone away.
One last dance with the autumn sun.
I don't know where you're going, but I know what you'll become.

TILL THE END

There is light within the blinding dark.
I see you. I am coming.
Life remains amidst the fading sparks.
We will not be forgotten.
There's still fight within your broken heart.
I understand; keep loving.
I'll ignite to make this end a start.
I'm with you—don't stop running.

Readington, New Jersey

THE FALL

One breath of moonlight turns my sunlit heart black.
Swallowed by the night, I am dead as winter, void of life.
I call to you from the darkest corner of the forest.
I beg for you to warm my frozen heart.
But the echoes of autumn are too loud;
I am lost while you are found.
I reach for no one.
The shadows of the forgotten take my hand
and we dance and we dance till I become one of them.

Round Valley Reservoir, Clinton, New Jersey

Olympic National Park, Washington

GRAINS

I scream, I fight, I break everything.
But I am given nothing.
I recede into silence, I remove myself from this shame.
Still, I am given nothing.
People can change, but sometimes they won't.
And I'll be damned if I'm blamed for what you do and what you don't.
I go back to what I know; I rise above your reign of rust.
To the life I lead that's built upon one thousand grains of love.
When history recalls the sorry outcome of this game,
the future will applaud and rise for those who refused to play.

EYES UP

When innocence is measured by need, and rights are stripped for comfort; when our entitled spirits grow without objection—we will find ourselves in a world scorched and barren.
Do not ask why. Do not ask how.
We did this to ourselves—we lost while looking down.

REVOLVE

When the red sun crests the horizon,
our dying dissent is set aflame.
A sacrifice for an aftermath graced
by our beautiful rage.

Rialto Beach, Clallam, Washington

STORMBORN

Lightning strikes my thunderous heart.
You thought this was over, but it is just the start.
My words will sear a home into the back of your mind.
My screams will echo into the hole where you hide.
Etched in blood, beating flesh, your heart will forever bear my name.
I am the voice you hear in the rain.

WITHIN THE DIVIDE

I no longer see the sun.
Only wreckage from the storm false gods cast upon us.
We were promised love,
and given divides.
Fences made of fire separate the you's from the I's.
My patience has expired.
I look into your eyes—one smile parts the swirling skies.
I see the sun again.
Rebirthed and awoken, alive and unbroken.
We are now the fire that cannot be silenced.

Cory Pass, Banff National Park, Alberta, Canada

THE GAME

The storm that rages on has struck us down with bolts of fire,
dividing hearts and stealing love till rage becomes desire.

SCORCHED

I will ascend beyond.
I will leap over mountains
into morning's dawn.
When the pale sun blinds
those looking down,
in the ashes of what's lost,
I will be found.

THE DUEL

Everything and nothing. That is what you give.
Simplicity has gone away and in its place you sit.
Waiting for my move, I wait more patiently for yours.
A tug of war for something that was never ours to hold.
Perhaps we'll rip ourselves in two—or just the hope we clutch too tight.
I've been here before.
I know the score.
There will be no victors in this fight.

Deception Pass, Washington

REVOLT

When we lose our minds to the flames, the floods, and the famine.
When the bugs learn to outwit, out power, and outlast us.
When we realize we can't breathe underwater and that the ocean always wins.
Don't look back and wonder how.
Don't look back and ask why.
When they ask why we cry, the simple reply
is that we did nothing and the sun burnt us blind.

Lake Minnewanka, Banff National Park, Alberta, Canada

NORDEN

If you listen you can almost hear the ocean from our yesteryears.
A rumbling sigh, for you and I, that whispers, "You are safe here."

Herring Cove, Campobello Island, Canada

Lake Cushman, Hoodsport, Washington

THE WHY

I remember a time when I was whole,
a time before the disintegration of my tender bones.
And then I wonder: Why?
Why do I stay?
Why do I let the world shake me blind and then swear I'm okay?
An exploration beyond the here and now to discover what's left of me after the explosion; after my heart crumbled into one thousand tiny pieces and blew away with the wind. A discovery of the past and how it shaped me into this creature; one that claws at the darkness, but refuses to let light in. I wonder why I see each goodbye as a loss, instead of a chance to learn and love again. And why do I only feel the cold on a sunny, winter day?
Why do I stay?
Perhaps I cannot leave until I appreciate the cold.
Perhaps I'll be no better elsewhere until I learn how to love while letting go.
If I cannot be happy in my darkness, I will not value the light.
In the shadows, I must grow, and if I stay, perhaps I might.

THE GIVER

I traded my soul to the wind.
It asked for nothing, still I gave it everything.
I gave my heart to the darkest black.
Night came and went, still I never asked for it back.
I lost my mind to the violent light.
Blind and burnt, I carried on without sight.
I asked the waning moon for help.
It said, "You must look within yourself."
I searched through what was left of me
and found myself in the holes of who I used to be.
Always there. Always brave.
Alive in the spaces that once were graves.
Reborn, my pieces are ablaze.
In the end, the giver always gets more than what they gave.

Bow Lake, Banff National Park, Alberta, Canada

THE SCULPTOR

I found a safe place for my reckless thoughts; a home where whispers take full shape.
Molded into something I can see, I am speechless, transformed, healed.
Beauty between the roadways—I give you all I have.
Every word hidden inside my head: my insanity, my chaos, my shackles.
Take them, sculpt them, give them a name.
Together, we will make the madness beautiful again.

Grand Canyon National Park, Arizona

Glacier National Park, Montana

CARRYING STONES

Through the woods where the wildlings roam—I walk till I find home.
A missed step, a lost friend, a call to the unknown.
The trees become familiar the farther I go
and I swear the sunlight sings my name each time I drop a stone.
Lighter than before, I suspect I'm becoming one of them.
These stones fall from my grip faster than I can comprehend.
Through the woods where the wildlings roam—I finally let go.
Of fear, of love, of what I've known.
In the afterglow, I am home.

WISH

On the wings of who I thought I was a wish clings to my spine.
To see, to feel, to breathe again.
To call this lost world mine.

Mweelrea Mountains, Ireland

RIPPLED

The afternoon sun is unforgiving, highlighting my rippled skin.
Every time I smile, a wave.
Every time I frown, the same.
I used to hate the way my flesh tracked the years,
but when I see your mirroring smile lines, love conquers the fear.
I am reminded how I got here—a glorious adventure filled with losses and wins.
Shine on me.
Each streak reveals how greatly I lived.

ADRIFT

Painted like twilight before the storm rolls through
—a star blossom battling her wildfire blues.
There for the chance to find a new world;
there thinking maybe her voice might be heard.
But as they do, the fates are cruel:
There was no one to listen, no one to care,
she had found a new nowhere with nobody there.
Just a lonely ocean
washing the shore
of the sadness that walked
along the beaches before.
The footprints were gone,
only the sea knew the names
of those who once came here
in search of the same.
A little lost, but hope still aflame,
she shared her secrets with the crashing waves.
A little lighter after letting go,
alive in the loss that had guided her home.

Cutler Cove, Maine

Glacier National Park, Montana

WILD WINDS

There's somewhere I ought to be.
Not with you, not with me.
I exit through a door behind the scenes
to a place where no one will look for me.
Worry not, the wild winds call my name.
When I return, all I've lost will be set aflame.
No longer silenced, no longer bound.
In the wild winds I am found.

ETHER

Again I find I am not here nor there;
I am somewhere in between.
I dance in a space that is infinite.

Haystack Rock, Cannon Beach, Oregon

ILLUMINATED

The clouds are on fire, illuminating my dark.
Light creeps upon the secrets I hide deep within my heart.
Reminding me of what I chose to keep.
Of what I left behind.
Of all that is lost.
Of what I loved that I can no longer find.
The road I took left me lonelier than that city of a million smiles.
The path I chose left scars on my cheeks where all the tears had dried.
If you asked me then, I'd tell you I never wanted to see another sunrise.
But with time comes grace and the chance to erase, to renew and start again.
Out of the dark, I come alive, more than ever before.
Without the dark, I never would have found what I was looking for.

INTO THE LIGHT

From dark to dawn, I come alive.
Brighter than day, darker than night.
I see you.
Can you see me?
—only in the light.
One more push,
I disappear.
Consumed by our final spark.
I see you.
Can you see me?
—only in the dark.

Ruby Beach, Washington

Petrified Forest National Park, Arizona

THE ROAD

I sometimes think about where I am and how I got here;
the road I took and all the turns I didn't take.
All the alternate endings never delivered—the happiness thwarted, the tragedy
averted, the bottomless pit of what-ifs and should-haves.
Imagination rogue, I force myself to pause.
I stop to focus on the here and now.
Present and clear, none of the maybes matter anymore.
Here and now, I will learn to love each moment as it comes my way.
Here and now, I will stop holding onto yesterday.

CROSSING WORDS

Drowning in the letters of a thousand broken words.
A terrifying maze, but I can feel beauty waiting at the end.
Ten thousand letters found and mended.
Up and above, where the solitary blend together.
As day takes the night, I am finally whole.
I see the light.
I am almost home.

Shi Shi Beach, Washington

Bull Lake, Glacier National Park, Montana

ROOTS & ROCKETS

I run from yesterday, it won't haunt me anymore.
Blind eye toward tomorrow, I release what I can't control.
I dive into the now.
Here we are born.
Here we come alive.

www.ingramcontent.com/pod-product-compliance
Lightning Source LLC
Chambersburg PA
CBHW060812090426
42737CB00002B/44